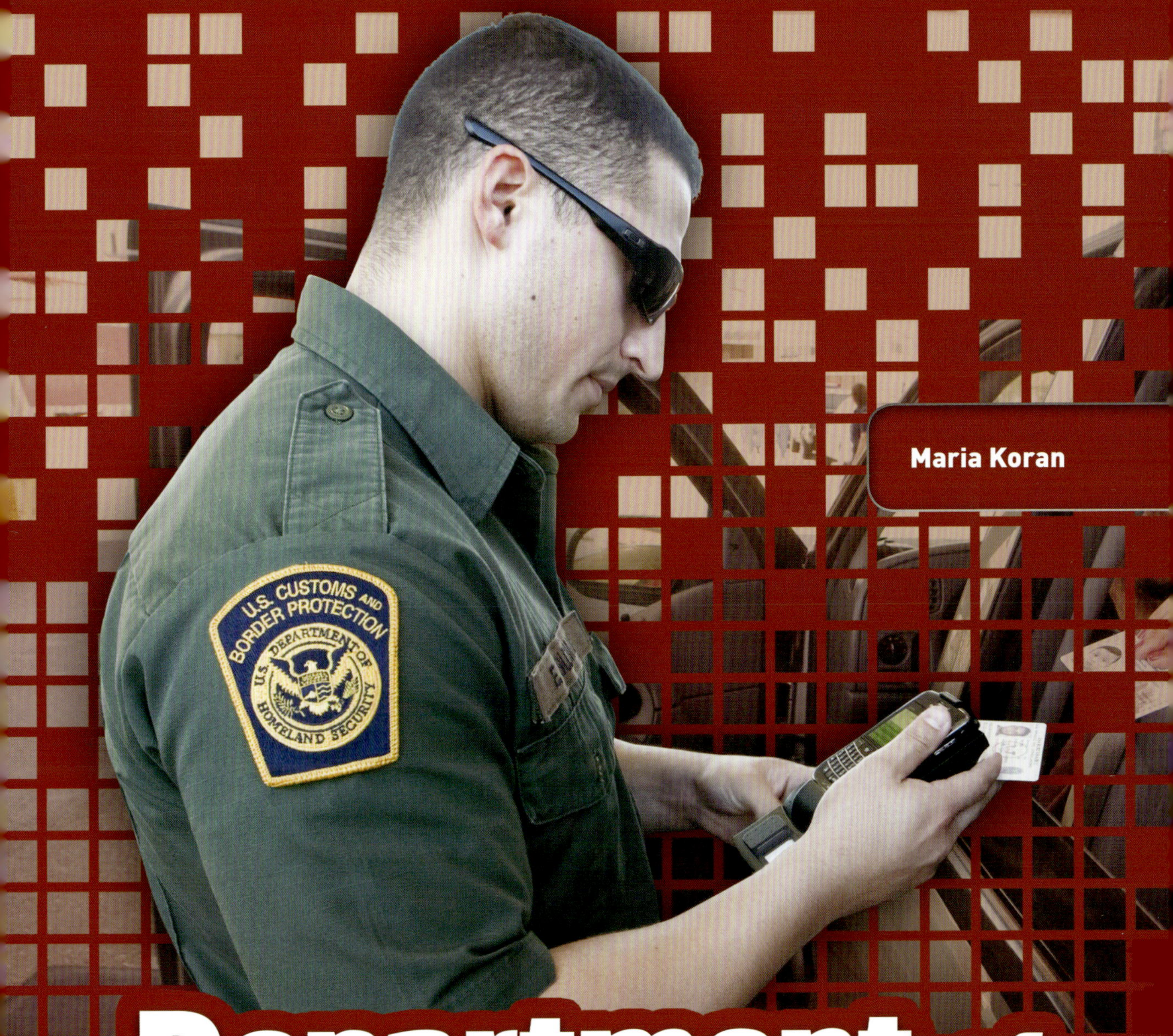

Maria Koran

Department of Homeland Security

POWER • AUTHORITY • GOVERNANCE

LIGHTBOX
openlightbox.com

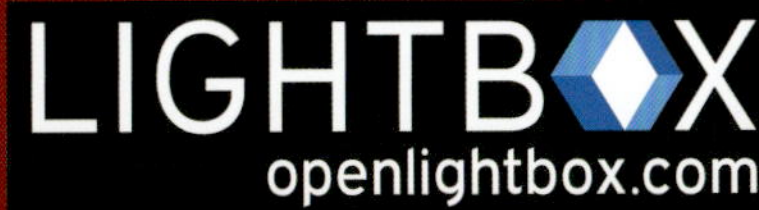

Go to **www.openlightbox.com** and enter this book's unique code.

ACCESS CODE

LBXP5742

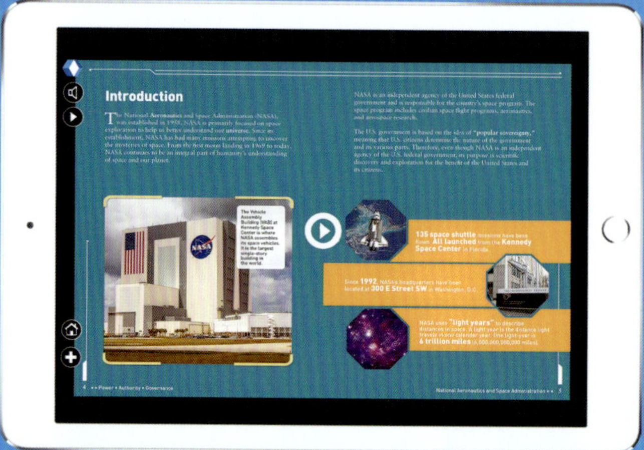

Lightbox is an all-inclusive digital solution for the teaching and learning of curriculum topics in an original, groundbreaking way. Lightbox is based on National Curriculum Standards.

STANDARD FEATURES OF LIGHTBOX

AUDIO High-quality narration using text-to-speech system

VIDEOS Embedded high-definition video clips

ACTIVITIES Printable PDFs that can be emailed and graded

WEBLINKS Curated links to external, child-safe resources

SLIDESHOWS Pictorial overviews of key concepts

TRANSPARENCIES Step-by-step layering of maps, diagrams, charts, and timelines

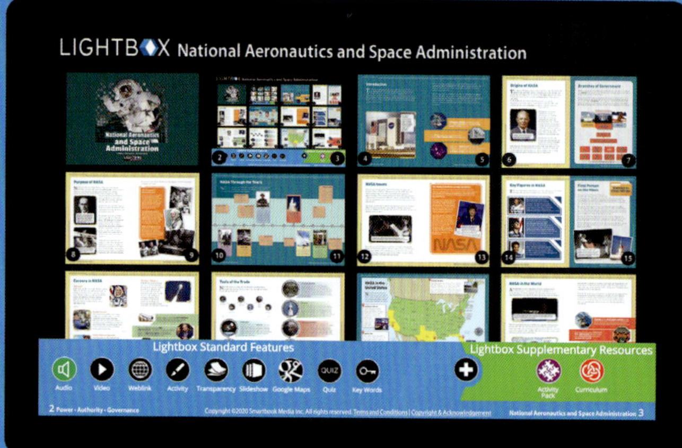

INTERACTIVE MAPS Interactive maps and aerial satellite imagery

QUIZZES Ten multiple choice questions that are automatically graded and emailed for teacher assessment

KEY WORDS Matching key concepts to their definitions

MORE Extra information and details on the subject

FIRST HAND Letters, diaries, and other primary sources

DOCS Speeches, newspaper articles, and other historical documents

POWER • AUTHORITY • GOVERNANCE

Department of Homeland Security

CONTENTS

Introduction

In late 2001, President George W. Bush looked over the structure of the U.S. government. There were agencies that had similar missions. He decided to join them into one organization. They became the Department of Homeland Security (DHS).

DHS is the third largest **cabinet position** in the **executive** branch. This means that it is a very big part of the government. DHS's job is to organize the activities of the 22 agencies underneath it. It tries to make sure that two agencies are not trying to do the same thing.

DHS wants to keep people safe. Its mission is, "With honor and integrity, we will safeguard the American people, our homeland, and our values." Its mission sounds simple, but its duties are very wide-ranging. DHS is responsible for everything from **terrorism** to tornadoes. DHS is a part of the executive branch of the government. This means that it reports directly to the president of the United States.

The Federal Emergency Management Agency (FEMA) is part of DHS. Its headquarters are in Washington, D.C.

The U.S. government is based on the idea of "popular sovereignty." This political principle means that the authority of a government is given to it by the people of that country. All parts of the U.S. government serve the will of the people. DHS has great authority and power. However, even it is subject to the will of the people of the United States.

DHS must be careful when doing any of its many jobs. It must always remember the liberties and **civil rights** of U.S. citizens. It must also remember who is a citizen. This is very clearly spelled out in the Fourteenth Amendment of the U.S. **Constitution**.

The DHS was created on **September 22, 2001**. Its headquarters is the largest construction project in Washington, D.C. The projected completion date is **2026**.

DHS is a huge department. The U.S. Immigration and Customs Enforcement (ICE) is just one of its **22 agencies.**

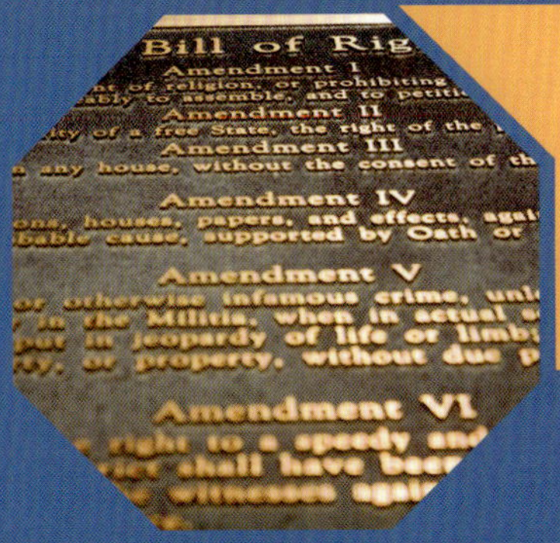

The United States Constitution is a short document. It has been increased in length over the years with **28 Amendments.**

Origins of the DHS

The Department of Homeland Security is a young department. However, many of the agencies that make up the DHS have existed for many decades. In fact, FEMA can trace its beginnings all the way back to 1803.

The DHS was created because of the terrorist attacks on September 11, 2001. Stopping another attack is the main purpose of the DHS. Government organizations that could contribute to national security were chosen to join DHS. Organizations such as Immigration and Customs Enforcement were among them.

President George W. Bush chose Pennsylvania's governor, Tom Ridge, to be the first director of the Office of Homeland Security. The office was in charge of, and organized, a national plan for security. Its main goal was to prevent any attacks in the future like the ones of 9/11. **Congress** passed the **Homeland Security Act** on November 25, 2002 and the new Department of Homeland Security was born.

George W. Bush was the governor of Texas before becoming president in 2001.

After Congress passed the Homeland Security Act of 2002, the Department of Homeland Security became independent. More importantly, it became a cabinet-level part of the executive branch of the government. The executive branch of government is the part that is responsible for making sure that the laws passed by Congress are "executed."

Branches of Government

The Department of Homeland Security is a cabinet-level post. It is in the executive branch of the government. Its leader in 2019 was Acting Secretary of Homeland Security Kevin McAleenan. Since DHS is part of the executive branch, Mr. McAleenan reports to the president.

The U.S. government is organized so that no one of the three branches has unlimited power. This system is known as "checks and balances." The idea is that each branch can "check" the power of the other two. This gives "balance" to the government.

Only Congress can make laws. Congress controls the U.S. government budget. These are some of the "checks" the **legislative** branch has over the executive. The U.S. Congress also has the power to investigate the DHS.

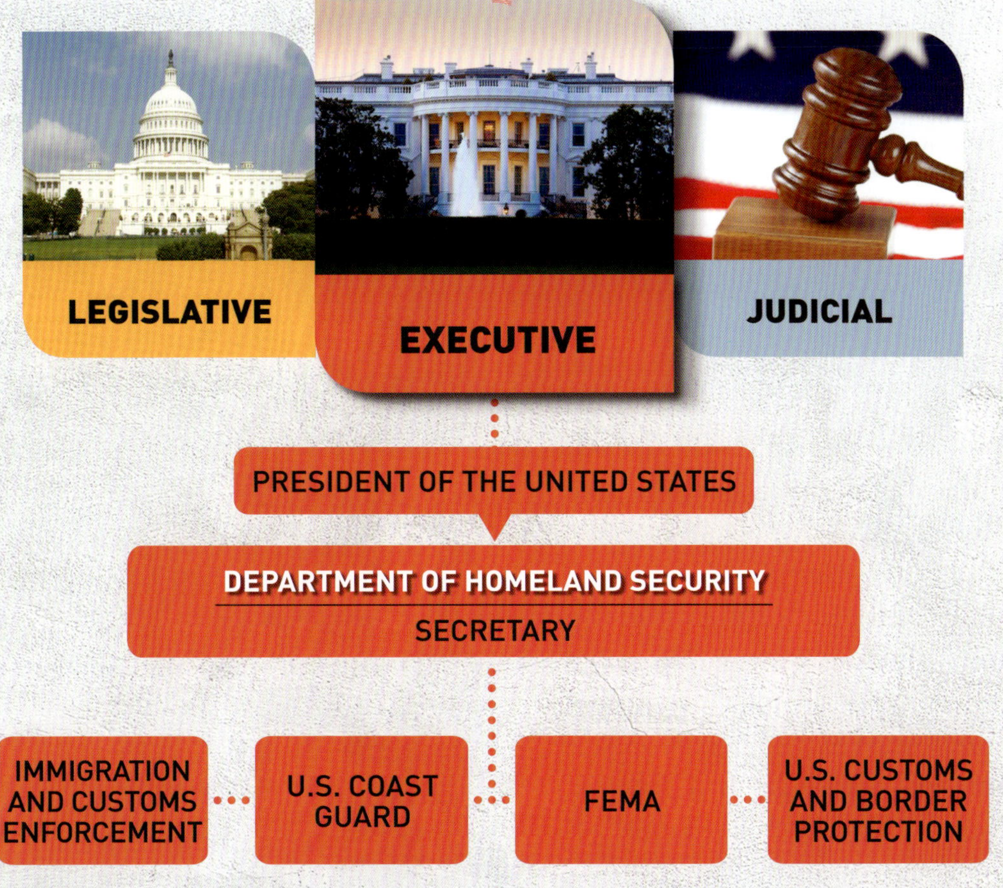

Purpose of the DHS

The mission of the DHS is, "With honor and integrity, we will safeguard the American people, our homeland, and our values." Its purpose is to keep us safe. Its job is to guard against any terrorist attacks like those we suffered on 9/11.

By combining different agencies, DHS can fight terrorism more efficiently.

To do all this, DHS has organized 22 different governmental agencies under one umbrella. This way, DHS can make sure that national needs are met. DHS does not want to just respond to a terrorist attack. DHS wants to make sure that an attack never happens. This means that DHS has to predict and disrupt potential terror attacks. This is difficult to do.

Unfortunately, terror attacks are not just done by foreign countries. DHS must also handle "domestic terrorism." That means that a U.S. citizen attacks his or her own country. An example of this is the Oklahoma City Bombing. On the morning of April 19, 1995, outside the Alfred P. Murrah Federal Building, a truck exploded. It destroyed most of the building. In total, 168 people, including children, were killed. Another 850 were wounded, and 462 were left homeless. The terrorists were Timothy McVeigh and Terry Nichols, both U.S. citizens.

The Oklahoma City Bombing was the worst case of domestic terrorism in U.S. history.

It is DHS's job to help people. But where does it get the authority and power to do this? DHS gets its authority from the Constitution. In questions of citizenship and immigration, DHS gets its authority from the Fourteenth Amendment, Section 1.

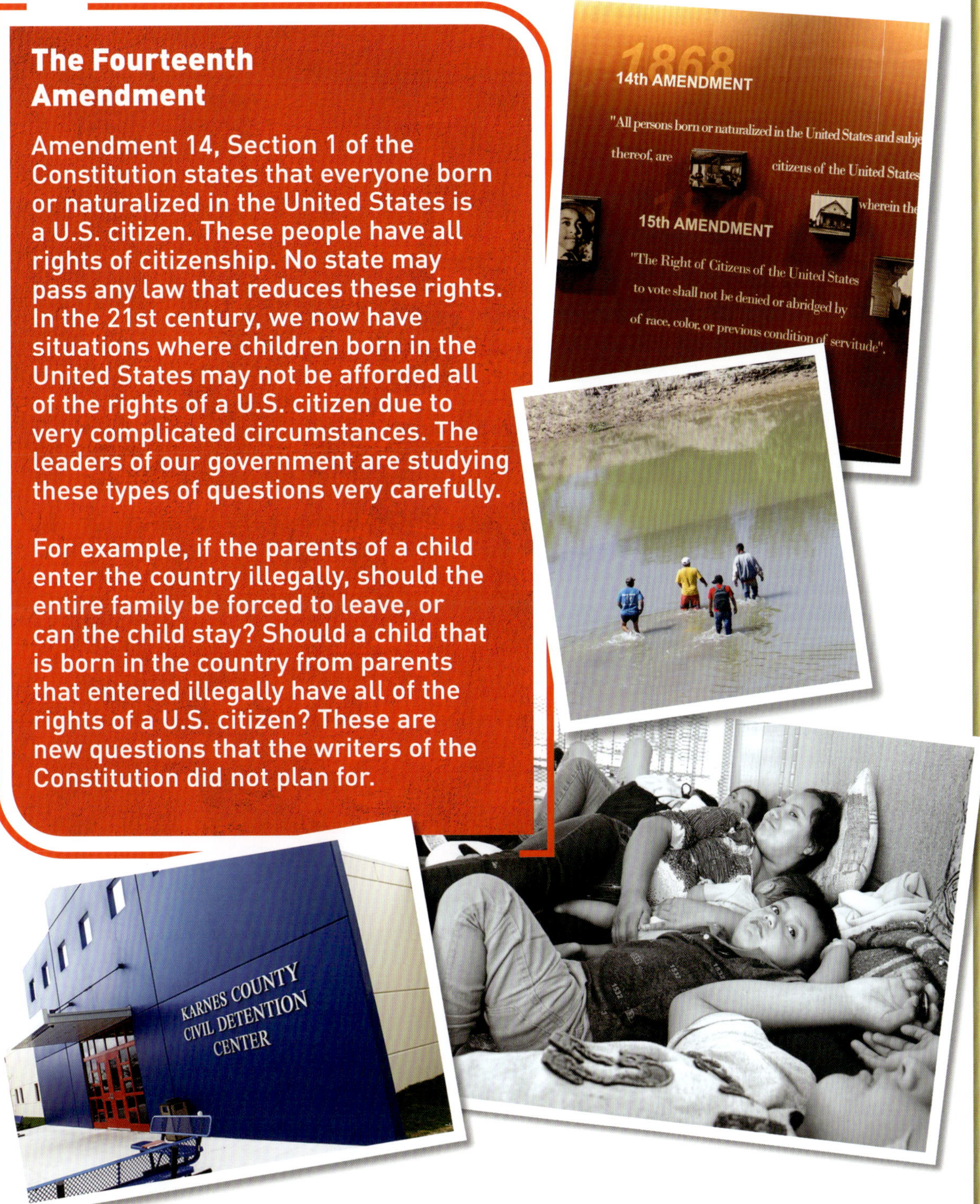

The Fourteenth Amendment

Amendment 14, Section 1 of the Constitution states that everyone born or naturalized in the United States is a U.S. citizen. These people have all rights of citizenship. No state may pass any law that reduces these rights. In the 21st century, we now have situations where children born in the United States may not be afforded all of the rights of a U.S. citizen due to very complicated circumstances. The leaders of our government are studying these types of questions very carefully.

For example, if the parents of a child enter the country illegally, should the entire family be forced to leave, or can the child stay? Should a child that is born in the country from parents that entered illegally have all of the rights of a U.S. citizen? These are new questions that the writers of the Constitution did not plan for.

DHS Through the Years

The DHS has only existed since 2002. However, since then, it has greatly expanded. It has had a major impact both at home and abroad.

September 11, 2001
Terrorist attacks on the World Trade Center, Pentagon, and one failed attack convince U.S. citizens of the need for greater security.

November 25, 2002
The Department of Homeland Security is created.

March 20, 2003
The second Gulf War begins. DHS plays an important role in keeping the country safe during this time period.

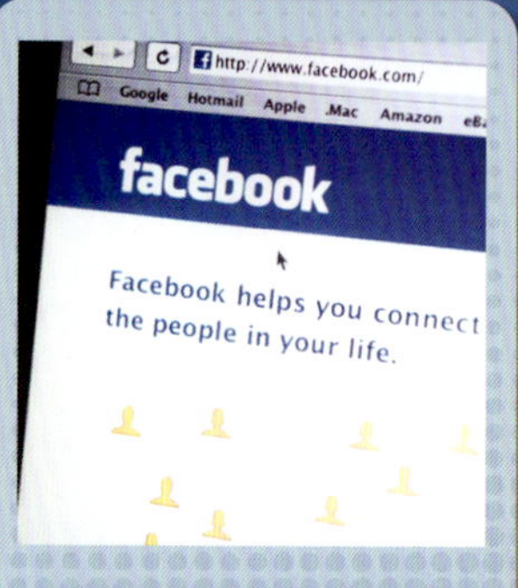

January 10, 2006
Facebook is launched. Online surveillance becomes a larger concern.

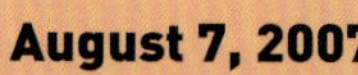

August 7, 2007
DHS takes over protection of federal buildings.

October 29, 2009
Director Napolitano reorganizes the federal protective services.

June 15, 2010
DHS joins the task force on intellectual property.

July 20, 2012

A gunman kills 12 people and wounds 70 more in a theater in Aurora, Colorado.

July 22, 2013

DHS takes a leadership role against human trafficking.

June 2014

The army and terrorist organization known as "ISIS" emerges.

June 2015

Two thirds of U.S. citizens own smartphones. Questions of tapping and monitoring by the NSA begin.

January 27, 2017

DHS begins to enforce a travel ban against citizens from seven nations with suspected ties to terrorism.

March 19, 2018

Edward Snowden begins giving televised interviews. In 2013, he had leaked classified information detailing U.S. surveillance programs.

DHS Issues

DHS agents risk their lives every day to protect the United States. However, recently there have been concerns about violations of civil rights. Some people who live on the border with Mexico are angry with the U.S. Border Patrol.

The U.S. Border Patrol must stop **immigrants** from entering the country illegally. The citizens of the United States are very divided on how this should be done and what force may be employed. Each year, DHS faces many lawsuits related to how it handles immigrants coming into the United States.

It is the job of U.S. Immigration and Custom Enforcement agents to enforce the laws of the United States. This includes the controversial travel ban that was proposed by President Donald Trump. According to the law, citizens of certain nations cannot enter the United States because their countries are heavily involved with terrorism. However, many argue that crimes committed by a few individuals in a country should not impact all the citizens of that country. This causes many difficult situations and choices for the DHS.

The United States has immigration stations for citizens of other countries that want to enter the country.

The United States shares the longest undefended national border in the world with our neighbor Canada. Many illegal immigrants in the United States are moving to Canada. They are being deported by the United States because they entered illegally. This is causing unusual friction between the two peaceful neighbors.

Balancing the Power of DHS

DHS and its agencies have enormous power and authority in the United States. They are literally able to put aside laws in certain occasions if there is a perceived threat to the security of the United States. However, like all parts of the U.S. government, there are checks and balances in place for DHS.

Both the **judicial** branch and the legislative branch have ways to protect citizens from DHS abusing its authority. DHS must produce information about the activities of its 22 agencies if requested by Congress. Congress also has the ability to pass laws that change how DHS is allowed to operate.

Citizens and organizations in the United States that believe they have been treated unfairly by an agency in DHS can also file lawsuits that are then decided by the courts that form the judicial branch.

Although DHS is a huge department in the government with very broad authority, even it must abide by the Constitution.

All DHS agencies must appear before Congress if requested to do so.

Key Figures in the DHS

Many notable people have made important contributions to the nation's safety while working for the DHS. Some helped create the department. Others helped run it.

Tom Ridge

Tom Ridge (1945–) was the first secretary of homeland security. Before that he was the first director of the Office of Homeland Security. He helped create the department's mission to protect the country against terrorist attacks. Ridge retired on February 1, 2005.

Michael Chertoff

Michael Chertoff (1953–) was the second secretary of homeland security. He served from February 15, 2005 to January 21, 2009 and organized the department into its current form. He also helped write the USA **Patriot Act**.

Janet Napolitano

Janet Napolitano (1957–) was the first woman to serve as secretary of homeland security. She became secretary on January 21, 2009 after serving as governor of Arizona. She helped create new security rules for airport travel. Napolitano retired from the department on September 6, 2013.

The Patriot Act and Civil Rights

HISTORICAL CASE STUDY

DHS was created in response to the terrorist attacks on 9/11. As part of the response to these attacks, director Chertoff and others created the USA Patriot Act. This Act was signed into law by President George W. Bush on October 26, 2001.

The rights and liberties guaranteed by the Constitution are a very important part of U.S. government and culture. Although the government needed a very aggressive policy to protect the country from any more terrorism, there were many people that felt that the Patriot Act went too far. Many people felt that, in particular, Muslim citizens were losing some of their civil liberties because the 9/11 attacks were carried out by radical Islamic terrorists.

Balancing civil liberties with the need to prevent another terrorist attack like 9/11 is a complicated issue. People on one side of the argument feel that a temporary loss of a civil liberty is justified if there is danger of another attack that kills people. However, there are also people on the other side of the argument that feel that it is a threat to the U.S. way of life if there is any loss of civil liberties, no matter what.

Today, the Patriot Act is still a law in the United States, but its power and authority have been greatly reduced since it was first signed in 2001.

Sections of the Patriot Act allow for searches without warrants. Many people feel this makes the act unconstitutional.

Careers in the DHS

U.S. Customs and Border Patrol

Customs and Border Patrol agents protect our borders. They have a lot of ground to cover. Agents ride on horses or in boats to go where cars cannot. They look for people crossing the border without permission. They also look for smugglers carrying guns or drugs.

U.S. Secret Service

The Secret Service is made up of officers, agents, and support workers. It has two main jobs. One is to investigate, the other is to protect. It looks for people who print fake money or use computers to commit crimes. The other job is to protect important people such as the president.

U.S. Immigration and Customs Enforcement Officers

ICE officers look for people who have come into the United States without permission. It is their job to find them. When they do, the officers start the process to send them back from where they came. ICE also employs lawyers and social workers. They work with the people the officers find.

Cybersecurity Experts

We depend on computers more every day. It is important to keep computer networks safe. The Cybersecurity and Infrastructure Security Agency (CISA) employs cybersecurity experts to look for possible threats. They also work on making computer networks safer to use.

In 2019, the DHS budget was **$47.5 billion**. Every year Congress must approve the budget amount.

The **Secretary of Homeland Security** is appointed by the president. The Senate **must always** confirm the appointment.

STEM stands for Science, Technology, Engineering, and Math. In **2016**, DHS had over **200** approved STEM degree programs.

Tools of the Trade

DHS requires many different types of tools and devices to do its job. Some of these tools are vehicles driven by officers. Other include weapons carried by DHS agents.

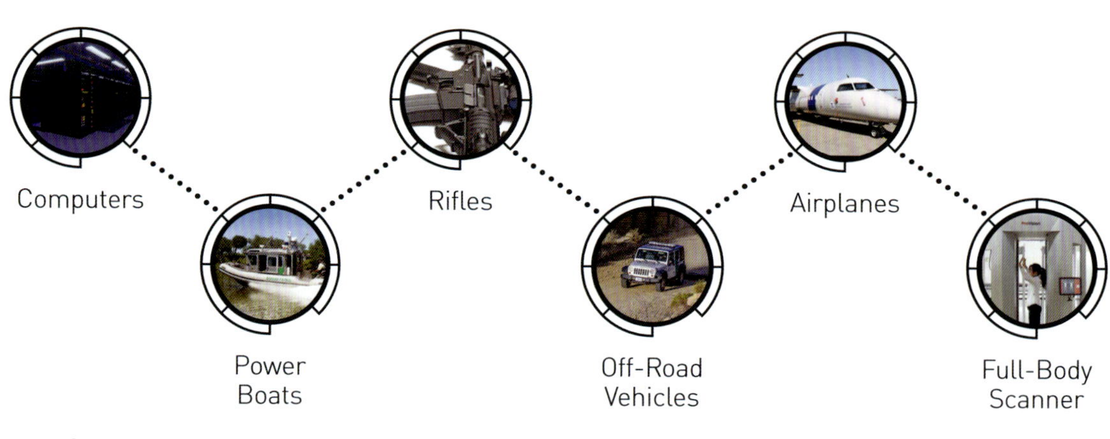

Computers

DHS uses powerful computers to store and analyze information. This information is used to find threats and prevent crimes. DHS computers contain information about countries and citizens from all over the world.

Power Boats

There are many rivers on some of our country's borders. DHS Border Patrol Officers use power boats to patrol these rivers. These boats protect the country from many dangers ranging from illegal immigration to drug smuggling.

Rifles

While used as a last resort, weapons are an important part of homeland security. A rifle is a powerful weapon. They can be used by Border Patrol agents to help protect themselves. Rifles are also used by Secret Service agents to protect themselves and the people they keep safe.

Off-Road Vehicles

DHS protects a lot of land. It needs vehicles that can drive over rough ground when there is no road. Off-road vehicles can carry people and equipment over terrain that normal cars cannot. This is important because these are often the areas where people try to enter the country illegally.

Airplanes

Aerial surveillance is an important part of homeland security. DHS uses airplanes to patrol areas it cannot get to on the ground. These areas can be over water or rough ground where vehicles also cannot go.

Full-Body Scanner

One of DHS's jobs is to keep air travel safe. It uses full-body scanners at airports to make sure people do not bring weapons or bombs on airplanes. These scanners are able to pick up even the slightest trace of suspicious substances and devices.

DHS in the United States

DHS works across the United States. This means the department must work with many different local agencies and organizations. DHS also uses each of its 22 agencies, such as FEMA, to help U.S. citizens.

1 San Diego, California

San Diego, California is where the first border barrier was built. In 1990, 14 miles of fencing was put up between San Diego and Tijuana, Mexico. The U.S. Border Patrol built it to prevent illegal immigration.

2 Las Vegas, Nevada

On October 1, 2017, a mass shooting took place in Las Vegas, Nevada. 58 people died and 858 people were injured. The victims were at a music festival. The shooter was Stephen Paddock. The Clark County Fire Department and Las Vegas Metropolitan Police were trained by FEMA to handle a mass shooting. Afterward, the government praised them for how they handled the situation.

LEGEND

- Land (USA)
- Land (Other)
- Water

SCALE

400 MILES

700 KILOMETERS

Pacific Ocean

New York City, New York

On September 11, 2001, terrorists attacked the United States. They hijacked four airplanes. They crashed two into the Twin Towers in New York City. Another crashed into the Pentagon. Passengers on the fourth plane fought the hijackers and it crashed in a field. The Department of Homeland Security was formed to prevent future attacks.

Washington, D.C.

On 30 March 1981, President Reagan and three others were shot on a Washington, D.C. street. Officers from the Secret Service, now a DHS agency, helped arrest the shooter, John Hinckley, Jr. Hinckley was put on trial and found not guilty by reason of insanity and committed to a mental hospital. He was released in 2016.

DHS in the World

DHS is in constant contact with agencies and governments around the world. They all work together on immigration issues, law enforcement, and trade. It is important for them to respect each other's customs and laws.

On November 28, 2018, the **NATO** Science for Peace and Security Programme and the DHS Science and Technology Directorate announced they would work together on a new project. Their **cyber** experts work together on ways to prevent terrorist threats.

In late 2018, large groups of migrants began to travel across Mexico toward the United States. The migrants were from countries in Central America. Immigration officials from Mexico and the United States work together to handle the large numbers of people.

Many caravans of migrants travel through Mexico on foot.

The U.S. Coast Guard patrols the oceans and lakes on U.S. borders. On January 30, 2019, the Coast Guard worked with the Caribbean Border Interagency Group to capture drug smugglers. They turned the smugglers and the drugs over to U.S. Drug Enforcement agents in Puerto Rico.

Officials at DHS know they must be able to work with other countries. DHS's main job is to keep U.S. borders secure and its people safe. To do that, it must work with people outside the borders, too.

Cyber experts from the **29** NATO countries work to counter terrorist threats.

Migrant caravans come from Central American countries. **Three** of the main countries of origin are Honduras, Guatemala, and Nicaragua.

The **U.S. Coast Guard** works with other agencies to stop smugglers carrying drugs. In **2018**, they recovered more than **one billion dollars** from drug smuggling.

DHS Today

The DHS today has many challenges that it did not have when it began in 2002. Many of these challenges are related to the huge number of immigrants that now try to enter the United States in many ways, and from many countries.

Because the DHS must protect us from foreign terrorists, they must have a way to know who is entering the country. In particular, they need to know if a person is coming from a country that is hostile to the United States, or if the person has committed serious crimes in another country. This type of information requires rigorous screening of the people that want to immigrate to the United States.

Some of the ways that DHS is handling this massive immigration challenge are very unpopular and portray the DHS badly, even while they work to protect the country. Because a parent may not get immediate entry to the United States as they are reviewed, families with children sometimes become separated. DHS is sometimes viewed as an agency that tears families apart.

Under President Trump, a travel ban has been put into place that prevents immigrants from coming from certain countries with suspected ties to terrorism. Opponents of this ban claim that it unfairly singles out these countries and their people.

Although large fences along the U.S. border have been built previously, in 2019 the United States began construction of an enormous barrier along our border with Mexico. This "wall" is extremely controversial with both U.S. citizens and other countries.

Today's DHS is working very hard to balance its job of protecting us while also being humane. It is also working to be much more transparent, so the citizens of the United States know how and why it makes certain decisions.

The Wall

MODERN CASE STUDY

One of the election promises made by President Donald Trump when he was still a candidate was that he would build a wall between the United States and Mexico to help with the problems of illegal immigration.

After being elected, President Trump worked to keep his campaign promise. The planned wall is extremely controversial and is causing a divide in the people of the United States itself. There are many people that are in favor of it, and many people that are against it.

The wall along the border with Mexico will stretch for hundreds of miles if it is completed.

The people in favor of the wall claim that it will help keep the United States safe from terrorists that enter the country illegally through the Mexican border. The people against it claim that it is inhumane to prevent people from entering the country if all they want to do is escape the problems in their home country.

The funding of the wall is also extremely controversial. It is causing many conflicts between the executive branch of government which is led by the president, and the legislative branch which is led by Congress. Both sides have very strong opinions on whether or not the wall should be built, and also how to pay for it.

There are many immigrants that enter the United States but are not processed by one of the border immigration centers.

DHS Looking to the Future

Today's DHS must plan for tomorrow's threats. This planning can be difficult. Technology and the world are changing very fast.

The speed at which technology advances can make it difficult to predict the future.

Technology might offer the greatest challenge. People all over the world are working on amazing projects. It is impossible to know what the next amazing idea will be. This is both exciting and frightening. Robots, flying **drones**, and **artificial intelligence** are just some of the many advances in technology. No matter what, it is the job of the people at DHS to predict what the future will hold.

To prepare for the future, in 2008 more than 20 government agencies joined together to make predictions. Agencies such as

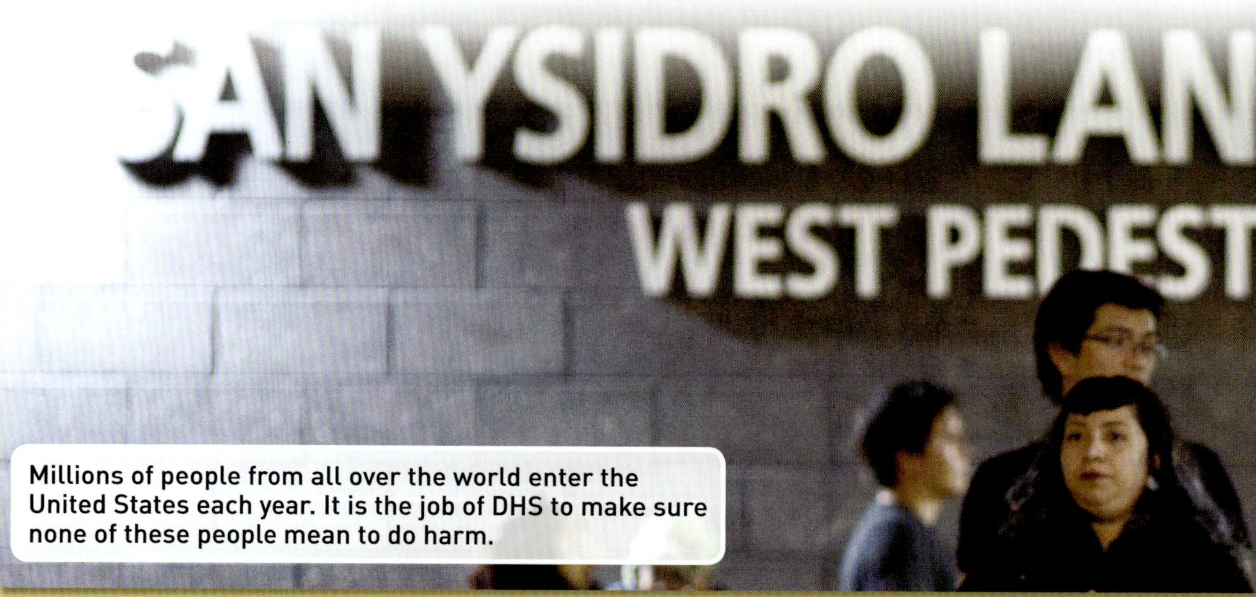

Millions of people from all over the world enter the United States each year. It is the job of DHS to make sure none of these people mean to do harm.

DHS understands that even the youngest U.S. citizens use technology. The department works to stay on the cutting edge of technology in order to help protect the country.

DHS, the FBI, the National Security Agency (NSA), and others formed the National Cyber Investigative Task Force. They want to defend against sophisticated technological dangers.

Changes in culture also make it hard to know what will happen next. In the United States, things are changing in unpredictable ways. One potential threat comes from the use of social media. Because of the growing number of websites and chat rooms, the U.S. cyber security must plan for future threats that might be organized using social media. A good solution is to attract younger people to join the DHS agencies. U.S. security teams want to have a young team to help them recognize situations with which they are not familiar. Although fighting terrorism is very serious, it is an exciting time for a young person to join any of the agencies that make up DHS.

ACTIVITY ★★

Create a Policy Paper

Unless you are Native American, your family immigrated here. The United States proudly calls itself "a nation of immigrants." Ellis Island in New York is a national monument. Immigration and immigration policy are very important subjects.

Today, immigration is a very "hot topic." Emotions are high on all sides of the question. Pretend that you are a member of DHS and it is your job to solve the problem about proper immigration and procedure. It is a big job.

Develop your own thoughts on immigration policies and procedures. Write a policy paper that summarizes your opinion.

Step 1:

Answer the following questions to help you develop your opinion.

1. The Fourteenth Amendment states that anyone born on U.S. soil is a full citizen. Do you agree? Explain your answer.
2. Do you think that a travel ban should affect a citizen of a foreign country if their relative is a U.S. citizen? Are there exceptions?
3. What should be done with children born here if their parents came here illegally? Why?
4. What would happen if the United States removed all border barriers? For example, we can walk across the Canadian border. Would that make things better or worse if we could do that with Mexico?
5. What would happen if we prevented all immigration into the United States?

6. Should we restrict immigration into the United States from only certain countries? If so, what are those countries? Why did you choose these countries?
7. If we prevent immigration into the United States, should other countries allow U.S. citizens to enter their country?

Step 2:

Take your ideas from Questions 1 - 7 and write a one-page policy paper. It should explain the policy you think is correct about how to address immigration issues. It should also explain why. Include an introductory paragraph.

- Paragraph 1: What is the question?
- Paragraph 2: What are the issues surrounding the question?
- Paragraph 3: What is your policy on the issue, and why?

QUIZ ★★

1 How many federal agencies are a part of DHS?

2 What do the initials DHS stand for?

3 Who was president when DHS was created?

4 What event caused the creation of DHS?

5 Who was the first secretary of DHS?

6 What are three agencies that are part of the National Cyber Investigative Task Force?

7 Which amendment to the Constitution explains who is a citizen of the United States?

8 What are two of DHS's "tools of the trade"?

9 If completed, "the wall" will be on the border of which U.S. neighbor?

10 What is one career choice with DHS?

ANSWERS

1. 22 2. Department of Homeland Security 3. George W. Bush 4. The September 11 attacks 5. Tom Ridge 6. DHS, FBI, NSA 7. The Fourteenth Amendment 8. Computer, power boat, rifle, jeep, airplane, body scanner 9. Mexico 10. Customs and border patrol, secret service, ICE, cybersecurity

KEY WORDS ★★

artificial intelligence: intelligence demonstrated by machines

cabinet position: an appointed officer of a department in the executive branch of the federal government of the United States

civil rights: the rights of citizens of a country to political and social freedom, and equality

Congress: governing body of the legislative branch of government consisting of two chambers, the House of Representatives and the Senate

Constitution: the supreme law of the United States of America

cyber: relating to computers, information technology, and virtual reality

drones: unmanned flying vehicles

executive: exercises authority and responsibility for the governance of a state. The power of the executive branch falls on the president of the United States.

Homeland Security Act: act that created the Department of Homeland Security

immigrants: people who live permanently in a foreign country

judicial: something that relates to a court or judge

legislative: a group of people with the authority to make laws for a political entity, such as a country or city

NATO: North Atlantic Treaty Organization, which consists of 29 member states from North America and Europe

Patriot Act: allows the federal government greater authority in tracking and intercepting communications for purposes of law enforcement and foreign intelligence.

terrorism: the use of violence and intimidation, especially against civilians, for political reasons

INDEX ★★

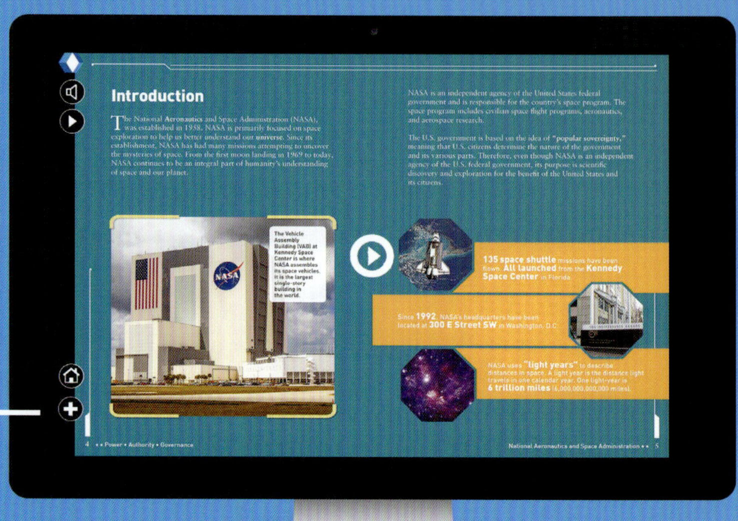

SUPPLEMENTARY RESOURCES

Click on the plus icon found in the bottom left corner of each spread to open additional teacher resources.

- Download and print the book's quizzes and activities
- Access curriculum correlations
- Explore additional web applications that enhance the Lightbox experience

LIGHTBOX DIGITAL TITLES

Packed full of integrated media

VIDEOS

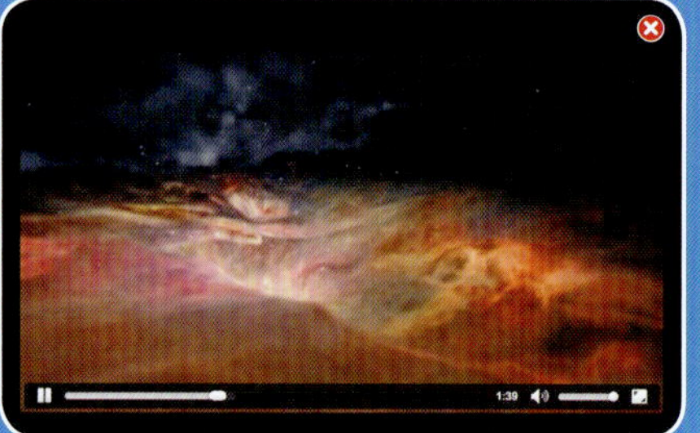

INTERACTIVE MAPS

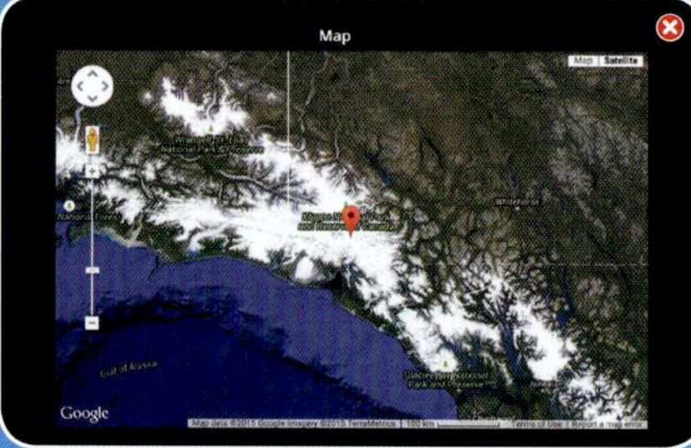

WEBLINKS

SLIDESHOWS

QUIZZES

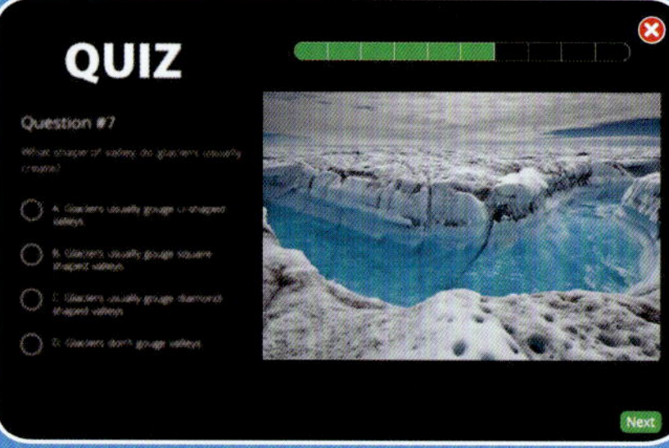

OPTIMIZED FOR

- ✔ TABLETS
- ✔ WHITEBOARDS
- ✔ COMPUTERS
- ✔ AND MUCH MORE!

Published by Smartbook Media Inc.
350 5th Avenue, 59th Floor New York, NY 10118
Website: www.openlightbox.com

Library of Congress Control Number: 2019939794

ISBN 978-1-5105-4683-7 (hardcover)
ISBN 978-1-5105-4684-4 (multi-user eBook)

Printed in Guangzhou, China
1 2 3 4 5 6 7 8 9 0 23 22 21 20 19

052019
122718

Editor: John Willis
Art Director: Terry Paulhus

Every reasonable effort has been made to trace ownership and to obtain permission to reprint copyright material. The publisher would be pleased to have any errors or omissions brought to its attention so that they may be corrected in subsequent printings.

The publisher acknowledges Alamy, Newscom, Shutterstock, and Wikimedia Commons as its primary image suppliers for this title.